THE ART
OF
HOVENWEEP

Ian Thompson

NOT FOR RESALE
This is a Free Book
Bookthing.org

Canyonlands Natural History Association, Moab, Utah

Copyright 2004, Canyonlands Natural History Association, Moab, Utah 84532
All rights reserved.
Library of Congress Catalog Number 92-83789
ISBN 0-937407-06-2

Includes bibliography.

The following granted permission to quote from the works indicated:

Jenkins, Leigh, Cultural Preservation Officer, Hopi Nation
"The Hopi View," in The Anasazi: Why Did They Leave? Where Did They Go? 1991,
Southwest Natural and Cultural Heritage Association, Albuquerque.

Ladd, Edmund, Pueblo Indian scholar from Zuni Pueblo
"The Zuni View," in The Anasazi: Why Did They Leave? Where Did They Go? 1991,
Southwest Natural and Cultural Heritage Association, Albuquerque.

Ortiz, Alfonso, Pueblo Indian scholar from San Juan Pueblo
The Tewa World, 1969, University of Chicago Press, Chicago.

Sando, Joe S., Pueblo Indian scholar from Jemez Pueblo
Pueblo Nations: Eight Centuries of Pueblo Indian History, 1992, Clear Light Publishers,
Santa Fe.

Sando, Joe S., Nee Hemish: A History of Jemez Pueblo, 1982, University of New Mexico Press,
Albuquerque.

Swentzell, Rina, Pueblo Indian scholar from Santa Clara Pueblo
Personal communication

Design/production: Carole Thickstun
Illustration and cartography: © 2004 Lawrence Ormsby
Aerial photography: © 2004 Michael Collier
Photography: Pages 18 and 27, © 2004 Deb and Robert Jensen
Pages iii, v, vi, 18, 25 and front cover © 2004 Sam Wainer
Page 5 William Henry Jackson, Denver Public Library,
Western History Collection, WHU-296
Page 13, 15, and 33 from the collections of the Bureau of Land Management,
Anasazi Heritage Center

Printed in China
by Everbest Printing Company
through Four Colour Imports, Ltd.
Louisville, Kentucky, USA

Dedication

To Don Ripley and to the memory of Bess Ripley.
They introduced me to Hovenweep.

                                        I.T.

CONTENTS

FOREWORD

If you are holding this book, I probably don't have to tell you that
Hovenweep is a special place. What you may not yet know is that this
is an equally remarkable book, written by an even more extraordinary
person. Ian Thompson—Sandy to his friends and family—lived most
of his life in the Four Corners Country. In his own way, he came to
know Hovenweep and the region where it is set as well as anyone
who has ever lived. In *The Towers of Hovenweep*, Sandy helps the
reader see these archeological sites not simply as awe-inspiring ruins,
but as the vibrant communities they once were, and he places these
Hovenweep communities into the larger cultural landscape of the vast
Mesa Verde archeological region.

Sandy's life was something of a paradox: He was an intensely
private person who lived a totally public life. He was the editor of two
regional newspapers; a city councilman and mayor of Durango,
Colorado; a sought-after member of boards, commissions, and
committees; and a key figure in developing the Crow Canyon
Archaeological Center in Cortez, Colorado, which is where he and I
first got to know each other. But the professional role that he
cherished most was his life as a writer, and the topic that captured his
literary imagination was the Four Corners region. He flourished as a
writer because he drew spiritual sustenance from being on the land
and contemplating the lives of those who have called this area home.

Sandy spent almost all of his free time exploring the region's
mountains, mesas, and canyons. If he couldn't be on the land, the
next best thing was researching and writing about the area's natural
environment and its cultural history and diversity. This calling
developed when he was a young man, and it intensified throughout
his life, sustaining him until his untimely death in 1998. Despite
being a private person, he was no recluse, and he was happiest when
he was exploring the region with one of his many friends or,
especially, his two sons.

Sandy and I began to spend time on the landscape in the late
1980s. At that time, a team of Crow Canyon archeologists were trying
to inventory every ancestral Puebloan village in the Mesa Verde
region. To set some limits on this endeavor we arbitrarily defined
villages as large sites with more than fifty structures. Sandy was the
executive director at Crow Canyon, and, in conjunction with this
inventory, he was developing his own research interests in these
villages. He and I spent many weekends roaming the countryside in

search of these large sites. Upon finding one, we set about the analytical business of estimating its size and its period of occupation. The day would inevitably end with us sitting on a rock and contemplating the beauty of the setting, or wondering what life may have been like eight centuries ago, when construction at the site had commenced.

Sandy was indefatigable in this pursuit, and if I was too tired or too busy, he would recruit someone else and off they would go. His collaboration with archeologists at Crow Canyon and others resulted in an inventory of more than 130 villages. Crow Canyon archeologists continue this pursuit and have currently located more than 180 large sites dating between A.D. 600 and 1300.

Pueblo Indian people lived in the Mesa Verde region throughout this seven-hundred-year period, but the location of individual settlements constantly shifted, and there were several periods of population growth, and decline. Typically, people lived in small settlements—essentially family farms—occupied by one or two families. Compared with the 180 known villages, there are tens of thousands of these small homesteads scattered throughout the region. The small homesteads were built in all periods. In contrast, most of the villages formed during the ninth and thirteenth centuries.

The greatest number of villages were constructed during the thirteenth century. Decades ago archeologists felt that the Mesa Verde region had largely been depopulated by the middle of the thirteenth century, and they viewed the cliff dwellings of Mesa Verde and the villages of Hovenweep as among the last settlements occupied. We now know that this was not the case; instead more than 70 thirteenth-century villages were located in the area that stretches from Mesa Verde in southwestern Colorado to Cedar Mesa in southeastern Utah. Most of these villages remained inhabited until the late A.D. 1200s.

Sandy described this network of large villages as lying in a broad arc from Mesa Verde, Colorado, to Blanding, Utah. The boundaries of the arc were between about 5,500 and 7,200 feet in elevation. Here, good soil is abundant, and even today it remains the most productive agricultural area in the region. Below this elevational band, rainfall is too sparse for dry-farming, and above it, growing seasons are too short. Almost all the large thirteenth-century villages lie within the great arc that Sandy recognized. Smaller homesteads surrounded many of these large sites, and small settlements are found in the portion of the Mesa Verde region outside this favored zone. But Sandy's arc contains the largest sites with the longest occupational histories, and as such it was the core of the Mesa Verde archeological region in the thirteenth century.

Hovenweep lies near the center of this network of thirteenth-century villages, and it was a place that Sandy returned to time and again. As he describes so eloquently in this book, there are aspects of the Hovenweep sites that are unique. Chief among these characteristics is their preservation. The Hovenweep sites contain many of the best-preserved examples of ancient Puebloan architecture found anywhere, which is unusual because the sites are set in the open and don't have the protection afforded by a natural shelter as in the alcoves in Mesa Verde National Park. In part, this preservation is a testament to the expert craftsmanship of those who built these remarkable structures.

For the most part, however, Hovenweep sites are similar to the other thirteenth-century villages in the region. These similarities became evident as Sandy and archeologists at Crow Canyon conducted detailed comparative studies. Archeologists Bill Lipe and Scott Ortman have documented the characteristics these sites share, some of which include a canyon setting, association with a spring, prominent towers, buildings with multiple concentric walls, and division of the site—usually by the main drainage—into two parts. These common features indicate close contact and regular interaction among the people who lived in the region. The formation of these thirteenth-century villages also signals a dramatic change in the location and character of regional settlement, with earlier dispersed communities being located on or close to the best upland farmlands while the later aggregated villages were usually adjacent to springs in canyon settings.

The dramatic changes of the early thirteenth century anticipate the largest transformation of all: the complete depopulation of the region by the end of the century. Research into what caused this migration is ongoing, but studies conducted since the first publication of *The Towers of Hovenweep* in 1993 indicate that there were many contributing factors. The environment deteriorated in several ways

during the thirteenth century, including stream entrenchment, drought, cooler temperatures, shorter growing seasons, and a breakdown in the timing of annual precipitation such that moisture fell during unpredictable times of the year. All of these changes made farming more difficult. Conflict and violence appear to have escalated during this period, perhaps in response to agricultural shortfalls. Interaction among people living within the region was common, but there was a dramatic decline in the interaction between residents of the Mesa Verde region and people in adjacent regions. Finally, the transformation of thirteenth-century settlement patterns indicate that there were important changes in the social and political organization of individual communities and in the organization of the regional settlement system. Migration was the response to these and other factors, but depopulation of the region did not spell the demise of Pueblo people.

They resettled in areas to the south, and the Pueblo culture continues to thrive in these areas today.

There has been considerable research in Hovenweep sites and the areas immediately surrounding these sites, but this research appears in professional reports with limited circulation. In producing *The Towers of Hovenweep*, Sandy thoroughly reviewed all of these studies, and one of the great accomplishments of this book is that it presents such an informed, concise, and readable account of this research. In many ways, his synthesis is greater than the sum of its parts. His greatest gift, however, was his ability to recognize and communicate to others that understanding ancient history is about deciphering connections. *The Towers of Hovenweep* is an exploration of the connections between nature and culture, the past and the present, and continuity and change. It also illustrates the connections between archeologists and American Indians, who both, in their own way, honor the past.

Sandy recognized that human beings can neither fully experience the present nor imagine the future without understanding their history. Even when we don't realize it, our actions and dreams are rooted there. That is why gaining a better understanding of what went before was so important to Sandy. He knew that there are many ways of knowing the past, and he drew on both archeological research and the traditional knowledge of Pueblo people in writing this book. Sandy firmly believed that these different ways of knowing need not be at odds; instead, they work together to enhance the human experience. *The Towers of Hovenweep* isn't a long book, but I think you will find that it achieves this lofty goal.

Mark D. Varien, Director of Research
Crow Canyon Archaeological Center
Cortez, Colorado

Hovenweep National Monument was created by Warren G. Harding's Presidential Proclamation in 1923, which states in part, "Whereas, there are in southwestern Colorado and southeastern Utah four groups of ruins, including prehistoric structures, the majority of which belong to unique types not found in other National Monuments, and show the finest prehistoric masonry in the United States . . . that there is hereby reserved and set apart as a National Monument to be known as Hovenweep National Monument . . . "

Since 1923 units have been added and boundaries adjusted.

The units on Cajon Mesa include Square Tower, where the ranger station is located, Cajon, Holly, Hackberry, and Cutthroat. The National Park Service mandate is to preserve and protect the cultural and natural resources of Hovenweep and assist visitors in understanding the ancestral Puebloans who built the structures and their relationship to the surrounding environment.

Scientists still have much to learn about the people who once lived at Hovenweep and the natural environment that sustained them. Trails lead from the parking areas through the ruins at each unit, providing access to the best points for viewing the significant pre-European structures.

For two reasons, visitors are asked to remain on the trails and never walk on or enter the structures. The structures are extremely fragile and their natural setting is equally fragile. Living organisms hold the soils in place. Walking off the trails makes the soil much more subject to wind and water erosion. Erosion quickly destroys the natural environment and threatens the stability of the unique structures.

There may be fragments of pottery and chipped stone along the trails. Leave all artifacts in place, as they tell archeologists a great deal about the significance of Hovenweep in space, time, and culture. Pueblo Indians revere archeological sites in the Four Corners region as important milestones in their past civilization. Visitors should respect them as such.

Mesa above Hovenweep
and Negro Canyon

Abajo
Mountains

Monticello

491

Dove Creek

191

Blanding

COLORADO
UTAH

CROSS CANYON

Pleasant
View

MONTEZUMA CANYON

95

HOVENWEEP CANYON

CAJON MESA

YELLOW JACKET CANYON

191

262

262

Hovenweep
National
Monument
(Square Tower
Community)

Bluff

163

San Juan River

262

Montezuma
Creek

Sleeping Ute
Mountain

35

Aneth

262

41

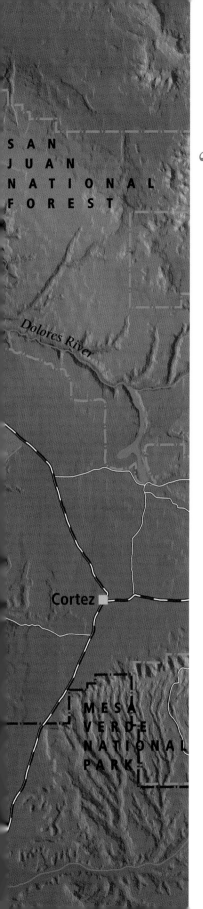

SAN
JUAN
NATIONAL
FOREST

Dolores River

Cortez

MESA
VERDE
NATIONAL
PARK

HOVENWEEP: TRADITION AND SCIENCE

"The people came from the north to their present areas of residence, from the place of origin at Shibapu (sipapu), where they emerged from the underworld by way of a lake . . . And with them came the Great Spirit, and He guided the ancient ones through the many arduous tasks of daily life. For unknown ages the ancient people were led from place to place on this great continent. Many of them finally settled at the Four Corners area, where they developed their civilization and stayed for some hundreds of years before moving to their present homeland. As the ancient ones relate, it was in order to preserve the people from total annihilation that the Great Spirit impelled them to migrate. This they did, in groups and in different directions. Thus it is that the people created new dialects. The country where the ancient ones lived was a vast open land of deserts, plains, and mountains. Here they built their villages and enhanced their lives. But they were filled with longing for perfection in their society, harmony with their environment, and so they moved from time to time to other places with better sources of food and a better environment. The Pueblo people built so well, and their culture worked so harmoniously, that they prospered. Their way of life spread over an area covering vast parts of the Southwest."

JOE S. SANDO, *Pueblo Indian scholar from Jemez Pueblo*, Pueblo Nations: Eight Centuries of Pueblo Indian History, *1992*

Community, change, and movement are common recurring themes throughout 2,000 years of Puebloan civilization in the American Southwest. Those themes are contained within the beautiful thirteenth-century towers of Hovenweep National Monument, a place that represents a brief but significant chapter in the history of an enduring and determined people.

Hovenweep today is remarkable for the stone structures clustered around small canyonheads cut into a sage-covered plateau. The setting is remote, beautiful, and characterized by silence. There were farms, 750 years ago, where the sage is now and the sights and sounds of vital human communities where now there is silence. The communities of Hovenweep were poised for change: the final movement of all Puebloan peoples from the San Juan River basin surrounding the Four Corners.

FINDING THE CENTER

From Cajon Mesa, where Hovenweep is located, one can look across the San Juan River valley and see the upper end of Black Mesa on the far southwestern horizon. From there, Black Mesa slopes gently southwestward to end in a series of bluffs overlooking the Little Colorado River valley. The villages of the modern Hopi Indians cluster on the edge of those bluffs and at the foot of the talus slopes below. The terrain between Hovenweep and the Hopi villages has its ups and downs, but there are no major barriers to foot traffic between them. It would be an easy five-day walk from Hovenweep to Hopi.

Pueblo Indians and archeologists agree that the Puebloan farmers who once lived in Hovenweep and the surrounding San Juan River basin are among the ancestors of the modern Hopi people, of the modern Zuni who also live in the Little Colorado River basin, and of modern Puebloan communities in the Rio Grande basin east of the San Juan.

> "Many Tewa elders* show a very detailed knowledge of the region north and northwest of San Juan into what is now southwestern Colorado. This is true even if they have never been there themselves. There are Tewa names for ruins, lakes, ponds, springs, and other prominent topographical features in this area. . . . such detailed knowledge does lend credence to the Tewa's migration traditions and claims that they once occupied an area considerably to the north and northwest of where they are now."
>
> --Alfonso Ortiz, Pueblo Indian scholar from
> San Juan Pueblo, The Tewa World, 1969

Migration themes are central to modern Pueblo Indian oral tradition. Hopis, Zunis, and Rio Grande Puebloans share this theme. Separate groups of people, of varying size, moved across the land, building and abandoning

---

* A major division of the Tanoan linguistic family whose pueblos are along the valley of the Rio Grande in New Mexico, except for Hano, which is in Hopi country in Arizona.

UTAH

COLORADO

Colorado River

San Juan Mountains

Hovenweep National Monument

Dolores River

Rio Grande River

San Juan River

Mesa Verde

ARIZONA

NEW MEXICO

Modern Zuni Pueblo

Modern Acoma Pueblo

towns, until they arrived at the places where they live today. The remains of those earlier towns can now be found scattered across the Southwest. Modern Puebloans revere those deserted pueblos as markers along their ancient ancestral migration routes.

Because Puebloan civilization is dynamic, it is impossible to conclude that life at Hovenweep resembled life in a modern Puebloan community. Some similarities do exist, however, and can be applied in understanding life at Hovenweep a thousand years ago. Puebloan civilization developed across a vast area of the Southwest, far beyond the San Juan River basin and, like European civilization, includes several different cultural and language groups which share some traits but which are unique in other ways. That has been true since the birth of Puebloan civilization.

REMEMBERING

Puebloan oral tradition and the science of archeology alike reflect a universal desire to retain and connect with the human past. While both Puebloan oral history and archeological research provide significant insights into the pre-European past of the San Juan River basin, there are important distinctions between the two. The particular oral history of each modern pueblo preserves knowledge of important past migrations and events and anchors the community to the surrounding environment. At the same time, it communicates with authority and certainty the symbolism, the high religious expectations, and the deeply held moral values of the community.

DISCOVERING

In contrast, archeological research attempts to free itself of values and to view the archeological record with scientific objectivity. Oral historians throughout the world pay less attention to measuring changes in decades, centuries, and millennia than do archeologists. To archeologists, defining change by units of time is the foundation of their research.

Spanish and European explorers beginning in the late eighteenth century made the first brief written descriptions of archeological sites in the San Juan River basin. The first mapping and photographing of sites took place in the summer of 1874 when the noted photographer William H. Jackson took time out from the Hayden Survey in the San Juan Mountains to explore the structures in Mancos and McElmo Canyons. The Jackson party also visited sites in the Hovenweep area.

Since 1874, some of the world's most prominent and influential archeologists have conducted research in the San Juan River basin, and methods and theories developed here are now applied throughout the world. This process of innovation in archeological research continues in the San Juan region today. While most of the structures in Hovenweep have never

Sandal of yucca fiber,
AHC collection

Somewhere in McElmo Canyon. Fortified Rock. William Henry Jackson photographed area in 1874 (circa)

been excavated, the archeology here is similar to that found elsewhere on the Great Sage Plain and on Mesa Verde. That research can be applied in interpreting the archeological record present in the canyonhead complexes of Hovenweep. Cross-cultural research, which examines similar cultures elsewhere in the world, is also useful in understanding the ancestral Puebloans of Hovenweep.

Archeologists constantly seek new methods for more accurately dating archeological sites. The most accurate dating method applied in the American Southwest uses the tree-ring calendar. Trees grow at a different rate each year, depending on rainfall and temperatures. The width of the tree ring indicates the growth rate for a year. Scientists have constructed an overlapping tree-ring calendar for the San Juan region stretching back more than two thousand years. Roof beams and other wood remnants found in sites are matched to the tree-ring calendar resulting in construction and occupation dates for the sites. One of the latest known tree-ring dates from a Puebloan structure in the San Juan region, A.D. 1277, was obtained from Hovenweep Castle in the Square Tower Community.

Archeologists can assign approximate dates to sites based on remnants of ceramics, spear points and arrowheads, and structures visible on the surface of the ground. All of these artifacts, when viewed in context, reveal a great deal about a site. That is why visitors are asked not to remove or displace artifacts and to avoid walking on walls and rubble. To do so is the same as ripping pages from the only existing copy of an ancient book. Every archeological site has more information to offer in the quest for a better understanding of America's remarkable pre-European past.

THE NATURAL WORLD: ANCHORING THE COSMOS

"The ancient Hemish homeland was a vast wildness of sparsely peopled, pinyon-covered rolling hills, flat-topped mesas, and deep desert canyons. From their homes they could see the snow-covered San Juan mountain range about forty miles to the north in present-day Colorado.

Today when opng-soma (war chief) recites the prayer-oratory, he includes 'the mountain range which the sun follows from east to west, the mountain range to the north, white with snow, the mountain range visible daily from the place of origin of the Hemish people, that mountain range which is hallowed by the spirits of our grandfathers.' "

--Joe S. Sando, Pueblo Indian scholar from Jemez Pueblo,
Nee Hemish: History of Jemez Pueblo, 1982

THE SAN JUAN RIVER BASIN

(left) Horseshoe Ruin may have been a gathering place, bringing members of surrounding communities together, assuring continuing integration of individuals into the community.

The San Juan River basin surrounds the Four Corners. The headwaters of the San Juan River are high in the San Juan Mountains near Wolf Creek Pass. The river flows in a westerly direction through parts of Colorado, New Mexico, and Utah and enters the Colorado River. Elevations in the San Juan River basin range from above 14,000 feet in the mountains to below 3,700 feet where the river enters the Colorado River in Lake Powell. The drop from the highest peaks to the lower river is nearly two vertical miles. Ecological zones range from those resembling the Alaskan Subarctic in the mountains above timberline to the Mexican Upper Sonoran across the lower mesas and valleys where Hovenweep is located. Snow and rain clouds approach the San Juan River basin from the Pacific Ocean. Rivers return snowmelt and rainfall runoff to the Pacific Ocean.

The basic geology of the San Juan River basin was formed by oceans and uplifts. Oceans moved across the region depositing deep sand beaches as they advanced and retreated and leaving deep limestone sediments upon their floors. The oceans retreated and the land rose. Erosion then tore at the uplifted domes of land and carried much of it toward the retreating seas. The process repeated itself several times and continues today. The last ocean advanced

*Little Ruin Canyon
with Sleeping Ute
Mountain in distance*

across this region about 100 million years ago and was gone by about
70 million years ago, spanning Late Cretaceous time.

The most recent uplift began with the retreat of the last Cretaceous
ocean, accompanied by Tertiary volcanic activity. The mountains in every
direction from Hovenweep are the remnants of the eroded uplifts, of
eroded deposits of volcanic tuff, or of igneous intrusions at the edges of
the uplifts. Two of the latest, smaller uplifts are visible from the roads into
Hovenweep. Not far to the east the horizon tilts gently upward toward
Sleeping Ute Mountain, and then drops into McElmo Canyon. That
upward-tilted highland is McElmo Dome. McElmo Canyon cuts through
McElmo Dome from east to west at the north end of Sleeping Ute
Mountain. On the western horizon the land slopes gently southward in
two giant steps from the Abajo Mountains. The higher of those steps is
Elk Ridge and the lower is Cedar Mesa. Both are erosion-scarred remnants
of the Monument Uplift. Sleeping Ute Mountain and the Abajos were
formed by igneous intrusion at the time the uplifts occurred. The Abajos
are more than 11,000 feet in elevation, and Sleeping Ute Mountain just
under 10,000 feet. All of these prominent landforms and many physically
lesser ones would have played an important role in anchoring and
defining the cosmos of the Hovenweep Puebloans.

The land plunges precipitously from the mountain peaks and ridges
until, at about 8,000 feet in elevation, it begins leveling onto the mesas,
which tilt gently toward the San Juan River. At about 5,000 feet the
mesas end and the land drops into the river valley. A large part of the
land area of the San Juan River basin is between 7,500 feet and 5,000 feet
in elevation. The mesas between these elevations have proven to be the
most favorable to farming since the first corn was planted in the San
Juan region more than two thousand years ago.

The San Juan River basin is bounded on the north by the Dolores
River basin, on the east by the Rio Grande basin, and on the south by the
Little Colorado River basin. At the same time as Puebloan cultures were
developing in the San Juan region, similar Puebloan cultures were
developing in the Little Colorado and Rio Grande regions. The divides
separating the drainages are, for the most part, low and easily traversed
on foot. It is sometimes difficult to know when one has walked from one
basin to the next.

THE GREAT SAGE PLAIN

The Great Sage Plain, where Cajon Mesa and Hovenweep are located, stretches over much of the northwest quadrant of the San Juan River basin from Mesa Verde National Park and Sleeping Ute Mountain in the south to the Dolores River and Abajo Mountains in the north. Viewed from the low ridge at the entrance to Mesa Verde National Park, where it was first seen and named by European explorers, it indeed appears to be a vast, unbroken plain tilting gently down to the southwest. This appearance is deceiving. The Great Sage Plain is, in fact, rent by deep, narrow canyons that run southwest toward the San Juan River, some more than a thousand feet deep. Between the canyons are narrow mesas that begin near the Dolores River and end in mid-air where canyons meet.

CAJON MESA/HOVENWEEP

Cajon Mesa, in the center of the Great Sage Plain, begins at about 6,800 feet in elevation, near the present farming hamlet of Pleasant View, Colorado. It slopes thirty miles southwest to end at 4,800 feet, overlooking the San Juan River near Cajon Ruin in Hovenweep National Monument. The caprock of Cajon Mesa, visible as canyon rims, is porous Dakota Sandstone, laid down in Late Cretaceous times. This sandstone soaks up water, which accounts for the canyonhead seeps that were so important to Hovenweep settlement patterns.

Cajon Mesa is bounded by Cross Canyon and Montezuma Canyon on the northwest and by Yellow Jacket and McElmo Canyons on the southeast. Cajon Mesa is cut along its southeast edge by numerous tributaries of McElmo Canyon. It is at the heads of these side canyons that the most visible remnants of the deserted Hovenweep communities are found. The canyonhead towers and residences date to a time of marked change for the Puebloan communities of the San Juan River basin.

Because it drops 2,000 feet in elevation, Cajon Mesa descends through four plant zones. Rainfall averages fifteen inches a year at the upper end of the mesa and six inches at the lower end. The highest zone is blanketed by pinyon-juniper forests such as those seen around the Cutthroat unit, located on the lower edge of this forest. Higher annual precipitation, cooler temperatures, and deeper soils characterize this zone. As the elevation drops, the pinyon pine ends and vegetation changes to sagebrush dotted by juniper, as on the terrain surrounding the Hackberry and Holly units. Next the juniper decreases and sagebrush dominates. This plant zone surrounds the Square Tower unit where the Hovenweep visitor center is located. The lowest plant zone is the shrubland surrounding the Cajon unit.

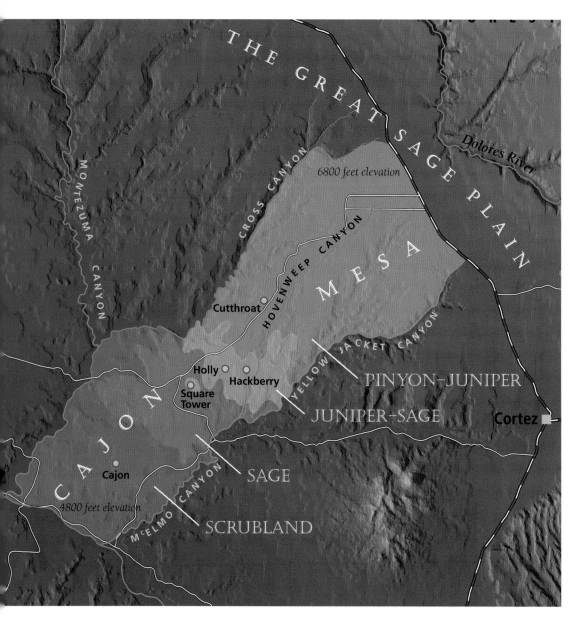

THE GREAT SAGE PLAIN

Dolores River

6800 feet elevation

CROSS CANYON

MONTEZUMA CANYON

HOVENWEEP CANYON

MESA

Cutthroat

JACKET CANYON

YELLOW

Holly

Hackberry

Square
Tower

PINYON–JUNIPER

JUNIPER–SAGE

Cortez

CAJON

Cajon

McELMO CANYON

SAGE

4800 feet elevation

SCRUBLAND

The topography of Cajon Mesa can be divided into six physiographic zones cutting across the four major plant zones. These physiographic zones include, in descending order, slightly rolling mesa tops, canyonheads with springs, canyon rims, canyon talus slopes, canyon bottoms, and arroyos in the canyon bottoms. Each zone supports its own ecosystem, and each played a role in the farming methods and changing settlement patterns of the Puebloan communities that once occupied Cajon Mesa and Hovenweep. The combinations of plant and physiographic zones allow a great deal of ecological diversity in the Hovenweep area. Puebloan understanding and manipulation of that diversity may help explain their successful tenure on Cajon Mesa.

CHANGING LIFEWAYS

"Over a period spanning thousands of years, the people were brought to a land where they were safe from the catastrophes of nature. There would be no tornadoes and no floods. Here in the new land they received their final instructions. The one above reminded them of their past trials and dangers, the sorrows and joys they had known together, and the strength they had demonstrated because of their unity. They were told of the necessity to plant and harvest crops for survival. They were shown the indigenous plants that grew wild and abundant upon the land. The food was plentiful. And so the civilization of the ancient ones developed around the planting of foods, more especially of corn. The systematic raising of corn led to the shaping of Pueblo religion, with rituals and prayers for rain and other conditions favorable to crops. The need to know the proper time for planting, cultivating, and harvesting led to developments in astronomical observation. They studied the behavior of the sun, the moon, clouds, the wind and the vernal equinox."

--JOE S. SANDO, *Pueblo Indian scholar from Jemez Pueblo,* Pueblo Nations: Eight Centuries of Pueblo Indian History, *1992*

The first people are thought to have entered the San Juan River basin about 11,000 years ago on the trails of the mammoths and large bison they hunted for food. These small bands of hunters, called Paleo-Indians, may have camped at the Hovenweep canyonheads where water was available from the seeps and where the sweeping vistas could be scanned for signs of game. The Paleo-Indians were highly mobile and left little trace of their presence at Hovenweep other than a few isolated projectile points.

The climate shifted, about 10,000 years ago, to resemble more closely today's conditions and the mammoths and large bison vanished. At the beginning of the Archaic period, some 9,000 years ago, the people in the San Juan River basin, like their Paleo-Indian predecessors, were hunters and gatherers. They pursued a more localized seasonal round than their predecessors, following elk, deer, mountain sheep and other game to the mountains in summer and harvesting roots, seeds, and berries there. In autumn they followed the game down to the mesas. Winter found the Archaic people camped in the warmer, lower elevations. With spring they turned once more on the slow journey toward the mountains, making temporary camps. They hunted with atlatls and darts and gathered food plants as they went.

The seasonal round is as old as humanity itself and may stretch back a million years or more before the beginnings of agriculture and the more deliberate manipulation of the environment. Some archeologists consider it the most successful human adaptation to the natural environment. All of us alive today are descended from the hunting and gathering cultures that, until recently, prevailed everywhere in the world. Within the San Juan River basin the small bands of Archaic peoples probably made much fuller use of the region's great topographical and ecological diversity than any people since.

Population density was low in Archaic times, in part because of the vast land area needed to support even a single small band of hunter-gatherers. Several Archaic campsites have been found in and around Hovenweep, the largest being at Cajon Ruin. Archaic camps

Agricultural axe,
AHC. 78.2.1368

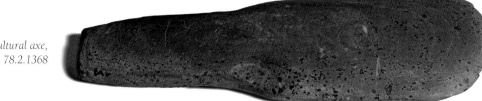

are characterized by burnt stone from hearths, stone tools, projectile points, and flakes left from making stone tools and points. Because of their mobility, the temporary nature of their camps, and their lack of ceramics, the Archaic people left little else in the archeological record.

THE FARMERS

Agriculture probably moved northward across the Southwest from Mexico. The shift to agriculture did not take place overnight, though considering the long duration of hunting and gathering, the new reliance on cultivated crops came quickly indeed. Why the adoption of agriculture occurred at all remains a matter of speculation. Hunter-gatherers may have seen it as a more stable means of subsistence when the climate became unfavorable to the seasonal round. Or agriculture may have been seen as a move, which, as populations grew, allowed hunters and gatherers to survive while continuing the seasonal round. The shift to agriculture was never absolute. Hunting and gathering continued to be important to the San Juan Puebloans even after a majority of their diet came from cultivated crops and domesticated turkeys. Wild plant and animal remains are found in even the latest San Juan Puebloan structures.

Agriculture first appeared in the San Juan River basin at least 2,000 years ago. Corn was the first crop grown, and it remains of tremendous importance to Puebloan cultures today. Squash was an early cultivated plant as well. The advent of agriculture marks the beginning of what archeologists called the Basketmaker II period in the San Juan River basin. The period is named for the finely crafted baskets made and used during that time. It would be several centuries before the first manufacture of ceramics. Semi-subterranean pithouses, in contrast to temporary Archaic camps, first appeared in the Basketmaker II period.

Only one possible Basketmaker II site has been found within the boundaries of Hovenweep National Monument. It is located at Cutthroat in the pinyon-juniper zone. Three more possible Basketmaker II sites have been recorded in the adjacent 4,000-acre survey area. In short, there was no significant Basketmaker II occupation of lower Cajon Mesa.

Remnants of an ancient basket, AHC, 97.10.SMT765.246. 1.7

The Basketmaker II period ended around A.D. 500, with the subsequent Basketmaker III period prevailing until about A.D. 700. Beans and turkeys appeared in the people's diet during Basketmaker III times, and the bow and arrow came into use. Ceramic manufacture was in practice by Basketmaker III times. Houses were large, deep pithouses with mud-covered roofs supported by large posts. Basketmaker III settlements usually ranged in size from one pithouse to a few, though there were occasional larger settlements. Population was greater and occupied a larger area of the San Juan River basin

Pueblo I bowl, Chapin black-on-white, Anasazi Heritage Center Collection, 99.16.5MT11861

than did the Basketmaker II population.

Only three possible Basketmaker III sites are known to exist within Hovenweep boundaries on Cajon Mesa. Six possible Basketmaker III sites were located in the adjacent survey area. The scarcity of Basketmaker sites indicates that intensive agriculture was slower in coming to lower Cajon Mesa than to other parts of the San Juan River basin.

About A.D. 700, the first contiguous surface structures began appearing in farm hamlets in the San Juan River basin. This marks the advent of the Pueblo I period, which lasted until A.D. 900. Surface structures were usually built of upright poles plastered with adobe mud. These rooms were joined in rows, forming pueblos. Despite the appearance of surface architecture, construction of pit structures continued.

In some areas of the San Juan River basin and adjacent Dolores River valley, Pueblo I hamlets coalesced into large villages of several hundred people. Large circular structures known as kivas served as activity centers integrating surrounding communities. The population was equal to or greater than in Basketmaker III times but was concentrated in smaller areas. The cultivation of cotton began in warmer areas.

Reconstruction of a pithouse, Basketmaker III period

Twelve small Pueblo I sites are located within Hovenweep boundaries. Seven small Pueblo I sites were found in the adjacent survey area. Not all the Pueblo I sites are residential; some served more limited uses such as pottery kilns and stone tool manufacturing areas. As in Basketmaker II and III times, lower Cajon Mesa remained nearly unoccupied in Pueblo I times. But change was in the air.

The Pueblo II period began about A.D. 900 with population dispersal from more densely occupied Pueblo I areas into surrounding, sparsely populated regions. By A.D. 1100, near the end of the period, the occupied regions were larger than ever before and the population greater. In the Great Sage Plain and on Mesa Verde, typical Pueblo II communities consisted of small, dispersed hamlets located on mesa-top ridges, well back from the canyon rims. Stone masonry appeared in surface room blocks and pit structures.

Cross section of a pithouse, Basketmaker III period

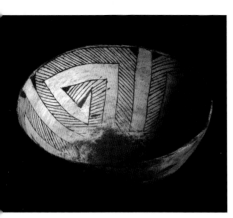

Traded vessel, note worn bottom. Brimhall black-on-white, late Pueblo II. From Chuska Mountains in New Mexico, found at Cannonball ruin, on edge of Hovenweep NM. Anasazi Heritage Center collection, 2000.17.5Mt338.RC4

Pueblo I homes, with kiva in center

Pit structures were no longer square but round and often lined with carefully shaped stone. These sunken, circular kivas may have served specialized social and religious functions in addition to accommodating many activities of daily life. Another change occurred in ceramics, with decoration becoming more elaborate and with some types being widely traded.

Pueblo II times saw the first significant occupation of lower Cajon Mesa by Puebloan farm families. Sixty-seven Pueblo II sites are located within Hovenweep boundaries and 127 sites in the adjacent survey area. Contrast this total of 194 sites to a total of nineteen Pueblo I sites found in the same two survey areas. Not all the Pueblo II sites on lower Cajon Mesa are residential sites, but those that are follow the pattern of small, dispersed hamlets atop low ridges well back from the canyonheads and rims.

Most of the Pueblo II hamlets on lower Cajon Mesa date to late in the period. By this time not

Reconstruction of the great kiva of Aztec Ruins NM (Chacoan)

only were nearby Pueblo II farm families migrating onto lower Cajon Mesa, but small groups of San Juan Puebloans may have begun migrating even farther into the nearby Rio Grande and Little Colorado River basins, joining similar Puebloan communities already there.

By Pueblo III times (A.D. 1150–1300), the population of lower Cajon Mesa was larger than ever. This was to be

the final era of Puebloan civilization within the San Juan River basin. Farming expanded from the mesa tops to the canyon talus slopes and bottoms. A total of 318 Pueblo III sites of all types have been recorded in the two survey areas on lower Cajon Mesa, another dramatic increase when compared to 194 Pueblo II sites in the same area and nineteen Pueblo I sites.

In late Pueblo III times, most farm families of the Great Sage Plain moved from the mesa tops to nearby canyon environments. The canyonhead complexes of Hovenweep so typify a change that it is often referred to as the Hovenweep Phase. The Cutthroat, Hackberry, Holly, Square Tower, and Cajon complexes of Hovenweep National Monument and other nearby pueblos all date to this time. Architecture became more varied and elaborate, as seen around the canyonheads of Hovenweep. This was also the time when the large cliff dwellings of Mesa Verde were constructed.

Top, Twin Towers at Square Tower group; bottom, nearby Painted Hand; right, Square Tower group.

(facing page)
Cutthroat Ruin is located in the pinyon-juniper plant zone at the highest elevation in Hovenweep National Monument. The amount of stone rubble near the towers indicates that there was once much more standing architecture. Unlike the other ruins in Hovenweep, Cutthroat is not clustered around a canyonhead.

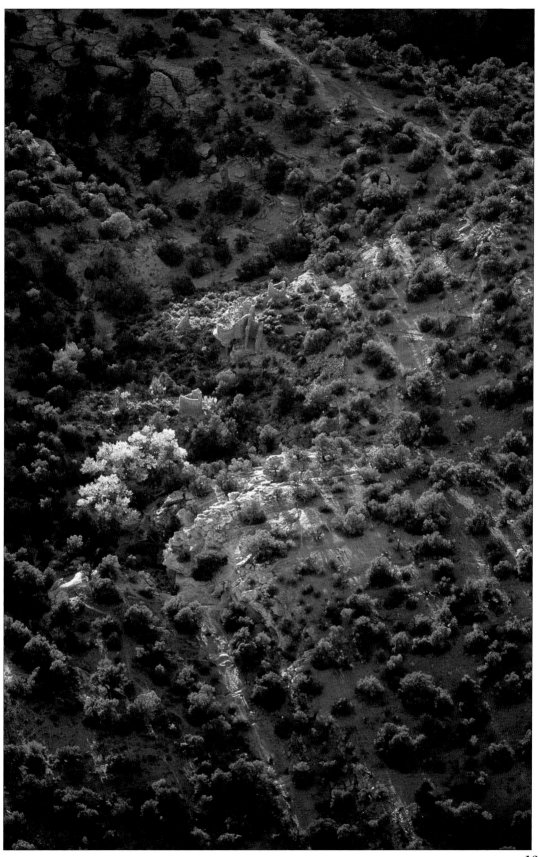

THE SQUARE TOWER COMMUNITY

66 *I think that Hovenweep is the most symbolic of places in the Southwest. I think that the people there then stepped into 'the masks of their ceremonies.' Hovenweep gives me a feeling similar to what I feel when I'm participating in ceremonies which require a tacit recognition of realities other than the blatantly visual. During those times I know the nature and energy of the bear, of the rock, of the clouds, of the water. I become aware of energies outside myself; outside the human context. At Hovenweep, I slide into the place and I begin to know the flowing warm sandstone under my feet, the cool preciousness of the water, the void of the canyon, and the all-covering sky. I want to be a part of the place."*
> *--Rina Swentzell, Pueblo Indian scholar from Santa Clara Pueblo*

By A.D.1270 most of the people of the Square Tower Community lived in a loose cluster of buildings perched on the edges of upper Little Ruin Canyon and, in places, nearly stretching across it from rim to rim. A seep, shaded by hackberry trees, is tucked beneath an overhang at the canyonhead a few yards from Square Tower itself. As the only permanent water source in the vicinity, the seep defined the community. That is, the families who had access to the seep and shared its water were members of the Square Tower Community.

(left)
Head of canyon, Square Tower Group

COMMUNITY

"Anyone belonging to the tribe of Nutria, cannot, even of his own fields, give land to any one person belonging to either of the other pueblos, unless that person happens to be a member of his clan. Nor can any man living at Pescado, go and take up even unclaimed land at Nutria or Ojo Caliente, unless with the consent of the body politic of the tribe which he wishes to join."

--Frank Hamilton Cushing,
Land Law and Labor, *Zuni Breadstuff,* 1892

Archeologists working atop McElmo Dome just east of Hovenweep point to evidence that the geographic boundaries of some Puebloan communities may have become fixed over time, but settlements continued to move around within those boundaries. People living within a particular geographical community would have had guaranteed and exclusive use of the farmland, water, and other resources contained within it. The canyonhead communities of Hovenweep appear to fit this pattern.

In all phases of ancestral Puebloan culture, there is evidence that communities composed of widely scattered hamlets occasionally coalesced into tighter and tighter clusters of residential units, finally to construct a single large pueblo or town. This town phase was subsequently followed by redispersal into small hamlets. The process was repeated on the Great Sage Plain at least three times over several centuries. Often the dispersing families built new hamlets over older ones vacated in earlier times.

Population dispersal may have occurred within community geographic boundaries when extended families and small groups experienced less need to share labor, harvests, and water with other community members. This was not necessarily a time of weakened ties to the long-established community. Even dispersed communities had centrally located activity areas that defined and integrated the community. The aggregation of dispersed hamlets into single, larger pueblos may have occurred when it was to the advantage of community members to forego self-reliance and to share labor, harvests, water, and other resources. The logistics of sharing would have been easier if everyone lived together in one place. On McElmo Dome, Pueblo II and early Pueblo III communities can be identified by the presence of one or more large structures where community members gathered and by the sparsely settled areas between the boundaries of one community and the next. Late Pueblo III settlement patterns at Hovenweep appear to conform to those found nearby with clusters of sites separated by sparsely settled areas.

Archeologists believe that in ancestral Puebloan communities political decisions were not imposed on the majority from above. Instead, decisions were arrived at by consensus, in which community

members reached collective agreements through discussions of issues. Cross-cultural studies indicate that it is difficult to maintain consensus if the population of the community exceeds 2,000 members. The population of the Hovenweep canyonhead communities remained far below that limit, so it is likely that decisions affecting the community as a whole were reached through consensus. There is little evidence in the archeological record that ancestral Puebloans sought power and status through the accumulation of property and goods. If anything, religious leaders may have been expected to forego personal interests entirely to concentrate on the well-being of the community as a whole.

Puebloan communities were not only egalitarian but each was autonomous, answering to no regional central authority. That pattern of autonomous small communities was maintained by the Rio Grande and Little Colorado River pueblos well into historic times. There is no archeological evidence to suggest that the Hovenweep communities varied from this pattern of community autonomy.

A few families in the Square Tower Community may have continued to live nearby on the mesa top, and a few more may have lived farther down the canyon rims from the major multiple residence structures visible at and near the canyonhead. Visitors to the Square Tower Community today, however, are most likely to notice Hovenweep Castle and Hovenweep House immediately surrounding the canyonhead and Square Tower in the canyon bottom. A short walk down the canyon rim are the Tower Point, Twin Towers, and Stronghold/Unit Type House complexes. The closeness of all these complexes to the permanent seep argues that they should not be considered separately, but together as part of an integrated community, though each complex might have been constructed by a specific group when it vacated a particular mesa-top hamlet and moved nearer the seep.

If we could travel back in time to the Square Tower Community in the early 1270s, we immediately would be struck by how much more architecture was visible then than now. Especially striking would be the number of structures built on the steep talus slopes at the foot of the cliffs and stair-stepping down toward the canyon floor. That talus slope architecture is most subject to being concealed by erosion and by vegetation. Talus slope architecture can still be seen beneath Hovenweep Castle, nearly spanning the canyon between Stronghold/Unit Type House on the north rim and Twin Towers on the south. Structures covered the slope to the south below Tower Point. In addition to the talus structures, the unexcavated rubble mounds attached to Hovenweep Castle and Hovenweep House overlooking the spring probably contain at least twenty rooms. Much of the stone masonry visible now would have been plastered over.

Canteen, Pueblo III, Mesa Verde black-on-white, 1200 to 1300,
Anasazi Heritage Center collection, 78.2.1747

An archeologist working at Hovenweep in the mid-1970s estimated that these complexes included about 200 rooms, a dozen towers, and numerous kiva depressions. In addition to the families living in this cluster of structures, a few more were probably living nearby on the mesa top and farther down the canyon rim. Although it is difficult to estimate population, the number of rooms indicates perhaps one hundred people lived in the Square Tower Community in A.D. 1270.

More architecture is not the only thing that would strike a time traveler to the Square Tower Community in 1270. Today there is a high desert wildness to the environment surrounding the complexes. At the time of occupation this would not have been a wild place but a more human, managed place. Square Tower Community was a farming village. In 1270, houses, granaries, fields, garden terraces, check dams, and reservoirs covered the landscape. The people were busy planting and tending fields, processing and preserving harvests, manufacturing ceramics and stone and bone tools, making clothing from cotton, feathers, and fur, preparing meals, renovating existing structures, building new structures, socializing, and practicing the religion deeply interwoven with all elements of Puebloan life and surroundings. During the summer some members of the community might have lived some distance away, next to fields located in spots that are more favorable.

Ancestral Puebloan projectile points from Sand Canyon

THE FIELDS

The soil covering Cajon Mesa was and is deposited by winds blowing up from the redlands to the southwest. It is fertile and retains moisture. Archeologists working on McElmo Dome estimate that in an average farming year four acres of crops per person, an area the size of two city blocks, would have been required to support a healthy population. This figure accounts for rotation of fallow land and a harvest large enough to store a one-year surplus of corn. Because the soil is shallower and precipitation is less at Square Tower than to the east, perhaps six acres per person would have been required here in an average year. Twice that may have been needed in a poor year.

Cutthroat Castle

Garden terraces stairstepped up the slopes from canyon bottom to cliffs. And where the canyon bottom widens farther from the seep, fields would have been planted as well. Different crops were probably grown in these differing environments, reflecting the Puebloan genius for matching human needs to optimum natural conditions.

The people of Square Tower Community were dryland farmers, who depended on winter snow and summer rain to replenish soil moisture. They built check dams and reservoirs to modify the landscape and to alter the natural flow of precious runoff water to meet agricultural needs. In a dry year, the water from the reservoirs would not have gone far. The farmers of Square Tower Community must have glanced often at the western horizon, hoping to see the summer rain clouds advancing toward their crops just as dryland farmers on the Great Sage Plain do today.

Several types of crops were grown at Hovenweep. Plant pollen can last for centuries in archeological sites in the arid Southwest. Because pollen for each plant is unique, the plants grown and used can be identified by analyzing pollen obtained during excavation. Pollen from cultivated domestic plants found within Square Tower Community includes corn, beans, squash, and cotton. Domestic animals would have included turkeys and dogs.

Human as they are, Puebloan communities are not apart from nature. The Square Tower Community depended upon the wild environment as well as the managed environment for physical and spiritual nourishment. Rabbit, hare, deer, and rodent bones, in addition to domesticated turkey bones, are found in structures at Hovenweep. Pollen from many useful native plants such as beeweed, wolfberry, and milkweed has been found in structures and middens at the Square Tower Community. Some wild plant species were probably encouraged to the point of semi-cultivation. Others were gathered from the wild. Some wild plant species occurring at Hovenweep today may actually have been introduced to the area by the Puebloan residents of Cajon Mesa centuries ago. One archeologist suggests that the hackberry trees around the canyonheads may be descended from trees planted there centuries ago to shade the seeps.

CIRCLES OF LIFE

Modern Puebloan communities are surrounded by concentric circles of shrines. Similar shrines can be found near Hovenweep. The inner circle marks the world of human residence and farming. The next circle defines the world of wild animals and plants respected, hunted, and gathered by the people of the inner circle. The outermost circle, defined by mountains, other lesser landforms, deserted, earlier towns and hamlets, and places with water is the distant circle from which the people came. It remains important for its definition of the peoples'

Rock art occurs at several locations in Hovenweep. In the Square Tower Community a petroglyph panel is situated on the cliff face directly beneath Tower Point. It includes two bird shapes, a spiral, and a figure resembling the T-shaped doorways found in Hovenweep structures. The figures are pecked into the patina covering the surface of the stone. The patina subsequently re-forms over the pecked areas, a process called repatination. Two other bird shapes are less visible.

Nancy H. Olsen, an archeologist who studied Hovenweep rock art, says, "Prolonged use of the same location is inferred from evidence that the motif is remade in the same place several times and can be seen in different stages of repatination." Olsen concludes that rock art at Hovenweep is similar to that found at Hopi and Zuni. Its purpose may have been as visual communication reinforcing the messages relayed down through the generations by oral historians. At Hovenweep, as elsewhere, rock art seems confined to specific locations rather than being randomly incised into every suitable or available cliff and boulder.

past and the boundary of their present community. The farthest geographical boundaries of the Square Tower Community would have been some distance from the shared seep at the head of Little Ruin Canyon.

Buildings in a Puebloan community often face inward to contain the human sphere. Unbuilt spaces between structures frame vistas of the outer, nonhuman spheres. Standing at the canyonhead above the Square Tower seep, we can sense this outward framing—Sleeping Ute Mountain, sprawling in the distance—and inward focusing quality of the architecture. Humanness is enclosed within the canyonhead. The sense of enclosure was enhanced by the low stone walls that link structures and arc from them to the cliff edges and down the talus slopes at Hovenweep House, Twin Towers, Unit Type House, and Stronghold. These low features are found in late sites in the canyon environment throughout the Great Sage Plain.

The flat, bare rimrock stretching around the canyonhead between Hovenweep Castle and Hovenweep House might well have been the central public plaza where the people gathered for major social and religious activities. Thus the plaza might have been the center where a sense of community was continually renewed.

THE TOWERS

The architectural forms referred to as towers have come to characterize Hovenweep in the minds of archeologists and visitors. Towers began appearing on the Great Sage Plain in late Pueblo II times in association with residential structures. By early Pueblo III times they were found in association with a single kiva and often connected to that kiva by a tunnel. In late Pueblo III times, large towers were being constructed in isolation on the canyon rims and atop huge boulders that had broken from the cliff and come to rest on the talus slopes and canyon bottoms. These late towers can be D-shaped, round, square, rectangular, or the shape of the boulder top upon which they were constructed, as is apparent at Hovenweep.

There have been nearly as many theories offered about towers as there are towers. Suggested functions of the towers include observation points, communications structures, defensive structures, astronomical calendars, ceremonial structures, and food storage buildings.

Little excavation has been done at Hovenweep, but in 1976 limited test excavations were done in seven towers by San Jose State University archeologists and students. Three were of the late Pueblo II-early Pueblo III type, and four were later, dating to the 1200s. Joseph C. Winter, who directed the San Jose State project, writes of those four:

"The results of these tests were striking . . . a wealth of intact vessels, chipped and ground stone tools, structural associations, and pollen and flotation samples were recovered suggesting a multitude of uses for this simple category called "tower" . . . it appears . . . that the tower category is actually an architectural rather than a functional classification. Certain tower rooms appear to have been ceremonial rooms, others were grinding rooms, still others were processing or manufacturing areas, and others may have been cooking or living areas. Many of the larger towers are multi-roomed structures in which a variety of different economic, social, and ceremonial activities probably occurred . . . It is also apparent that the architectural style and uses of the structures changed through time, from the small, crudely built mesa top towers of [Pueblo II-early Pueblo III] times to the imposing multiple story towers of the thirteenth century."

The structures in Hovenweep were selected for National Monument designation for the quality of their architecture and their excellent state of preservation, not for their size. In 1270, there were larger pueblos located on the canyon rims of upper Cajon Mesa, at canyonheads atop McElmo Dome, and in the bottoms of Montezuma and McElmo Canyons to the north and south of Hovenweep. The total population of the Great Sage Plain within a day's walk from Square Tower would have numbered in the thousands.

One test was conducted in the northwest room of the west tower of the Twin Towers. Seven whole and partial Pueblo vessels were found on the floor. The floor was made of thick plaster set on fill with scores of human footprints molded into the plaster. Tree-ring dates placed the tower's construction at no earlier than A.D. 1232.

The northwest end of Hovenweep Castle is a D-shaped tower. Ray A. Williamson, an astronomer who has done research at Hovenweep, found that small ports in the exterior walls, an outside doorway, and an inside doorway combined to create a calendar indicating the dates of the summer and winter solstices and the vernal and autumnal equinox sunsets. Sunlight shining through the exterior openings strikes particular interior architectural features on those dates. This solar calendar was important in determining planting dates and in observing the ceremonial cycle. Calendrical features, including petroglyphs, are found elsewhere in Hovenweep as well.

To the modern visitor, the Square Tower Community may seem to be in the middle of nowhere. Members of the Square Tower Community in 1270 did not feel this sense of isolation. A few miles to the southwest is Cajon Ruin and a few miles to the northeast are the Holly, Hackberry, and Cutthroat ruins. All are within a two-hour walk from Square Tower. All of these canyonhead complexes are similar to Square Tower in organization and time of occupation. All represent the late aggregation from the mesa tops into tightly clustered settlements in the canyons.

In 1270, as at Square Tower, the mesa tops, canyon rims, talus slopes, and canyon bottoms in the Cajon, Holly, Hackberry, and Cutthroat Communities were a much more human and managed landscape than is apparent today. Towers and other structures cluster tightly around the canyonhead seeps, even more tightly than within the Square Tower Community. Low stone walls, still visible to the discerning eye, linked structures to one another and to the cliff edges. Fields, terrace gardens, and other agricultural features spread out from the community centers near the seeps.

Despite their similarities, the Hovenweep units are different in many ways. Not only are they located in differing plant zones, moving down Cajon Mesa from the Cutthroat to the Cajon unit, but architecture and layout vary from unit to unit. At Cutthroat one is struck by the number of kivas still visible and by the complex's location in the canyon bottom rather than at a canyonhead. At Hackberry the architecture nearly encloses the canyonhead. Nearby Horseshoe Ruin, resembling other large D-shaped structures found across the Great Sage Plain, invites speculation. At Holly, a tower perched on a boulder in the canyonhead is silent witness to the building skills and architectural imagination of the Hovenweep Puebloans. At Cajon, the canyonhead architecture frames a sweeping vista of the San Juan River valley, with Monument Valley and Black Mesa in the distance.

The boundaries of each of these communities were some distance out from the clustered populations and homes of each, encompassing community farming, wild-plant gathering, and small-game hunting areas. The amount of interaction between the communities is a matter of speculation but, given their proximity, it was probably frequent.

THE NEIGHBORS

Although modern roads must go around the canyons cut deep into the Great Sage Plain, footpaths can cross them. Thus thirteenth-century distances between the Great Sage Plain pueblos were much shorter than the routes used now. Within thirty miles by foot were the larger Mud Springs, Goodman Point, Cow Canyon, and Sand Canyon Communities. Communities with populations roughly equal to Square Tower would have included Cannonball, Seven Towers,

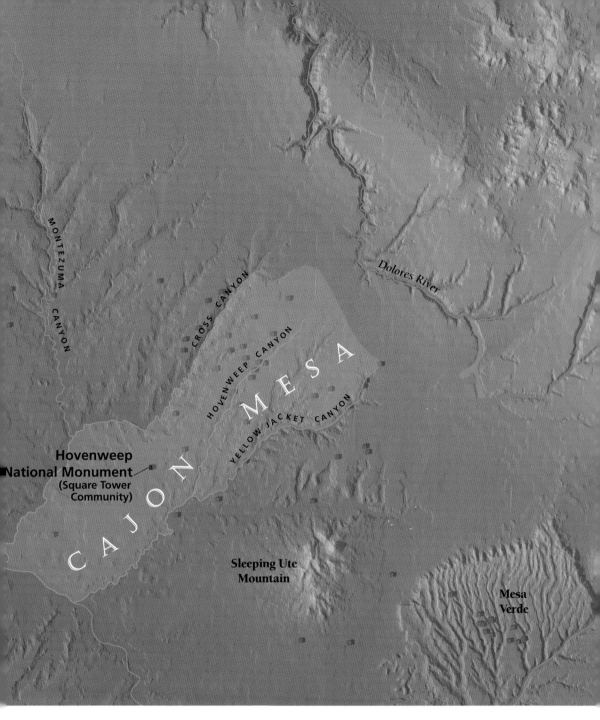

Easter, Miller, Woods Mesa, and Castle Rock. Numerous smaller communities were present in the canyon environment of the Great Sage Plain at the same time as the Hovenweep canyonhead complexes were occupied.

Several thousand acres of mesa and canyon farmland would have been required to support the population of the Great Sage Plain in 1270. Hunting and gathering areas would have extended beyond the fields. Wood for fuel and construction would have been harvested from within community boundaries. In short, much of the land area of the Great Sage Plain would have been managed to meet human needs.

MIGRATION: TAKING THE NEXT STEP

"The people saw that any achieved balance or coming together was tenuous. That is why clouds play such an important part in the thinking of the people. Clouds move, they play with the wind, and produce more rain, hail, and snow. They bring movement. They are movement. Why do we still identify with clouds? We become clouds when we die. We are always singing about cloud boys and girls. I think we do these things because we are supposed to move and change on a daily basis. Nothing ever stays the same. In that vein the people remained for awhile in Hovenweep creating the dark, interior spaces of the towers to balance the bright, strong, bouncing light of the canyon tops—stating their understanding of that particular place, knowing that they did not belong to that particular place but to the earth in general."

--Rina Swentzell, Pueblo Indian scholar from Santa Clara Pueblo

When first wandering among the architectural remains of the Square Tower Community, we are likely to be struck by the silence. The silence can be so overwhelming that it is difficult to acknowledge that this place was once a thriving farming village not so different from any small community. People were born here. People lived here. People worked here. People played here. People loved here. People argued here. People worshiped here. People grieved here, hoped here, feared here. People grew old or ill, died, and were buried here.

Then people moved from here. They took their memories of this place, and little else, with them. The village may have stood empty but it lived in the memory of the people who moved. It was still theirs.

(left)
Horseshoe Ruin

(right)
Stone with spiral design, Anasazi Heritage Center Collection, 78.28.5MT2149.119.7

Movements of people within community boundaries, and sometimes farther, had long characterized the San Juan Puebloans. The move from the Square Tower Community was not the same. This time the move signaled the end of an era. The emigrants from the Square Tower Community were not alone. All the communities of the Great Sage Plain, Mesa Verde, of the San Juan River basin as a whole, moved and ultimately crossed the low divides into neighboring basins. They probably did not move en masse but as small groups over a period of years. The curtain fell on living Puebloan civilization in the San Juan River basin at the same time a new era was dawning among the long-established Puebloans of the Rio Grande and Little Colorado River basins.

A SENSE OF BALANCE

Oral traditions about the origins of today's Puebloan communities, like the great origin accounts of all cultures, describe the creation of or emergence into this world, the creation of the first human male and female, and the subsequent movement of descended groups of people into and across the wilderness. Languages develop. Communities develop. Communities settle into one place and seek a balance, equilibrium, with the surrounding environment. Imbalances occur, communities move on, having learned from trial and error, and settle elsewhere. Disputes arise and factions emerge, dissatisfied groups leave to continue the migration, going their own way, forming new communities, stopping for a time to build and occupy new towns. Religion becomes the mediating structure uniting people and nature, uniting people and people . . . the source of balance, of equilibrium, if properly observed.

Loss of balance with the surrounding nature and society triggered the migrations of particular communities. The learning continued until at last the communities recognized that they had come to the special place where they were intended to remain. Sometimes a migrating group stopped at an existing village and asked permission to join it. If permission was granted, they stayed. If not, they moved on and built a new town nearby.

The oral histories of modern Puebloan communities recognize the deserted villages of the San Juan River basin, among others, as evidence supporting their accounts of the migration of ancestors toward the existing towns in the Rio Grande and Little Colorado River basins.

PUSHED OR PULLED?

The deserted villages and hamlets of the San Juan River basin have captured the attention of archeologists for the last century and much scientific research has focused on the causes behind the Puebloan move from the region. Until recently it was widely assumed that the people left reluctantly, even involuntarily. Specific explanations have ranged from the arrival of aggressive outsiders who raided the Puebloan communities to the effects of a great drought upon a people who depended largely upon dryland farms for food. The cliff dwellings of Mesa Verde and other areas were seen as defensive structures where the last peaceful Puebloans took refuge from the raiders.

PIII, McElmo black-on-white, possibly painted by a child, in imitation of the adult style, AHC, 78.2.1871

Countering the assumption that the cliff dwellings were defensive architecture is the fact that most San Juan Puebloans in the late thirteenth century built and occupied villages on the Great Sage Plain, including those at Hovenweep, where defense seems not to have been a major concern. The towers would have been death traps for people taking refuge in them. Also countering the aggressor theory is the relatively sparse evidence of violence exhibited in human remains of the period.

Some evidence of violence and physical trauma does exist in the archeological record in the area, but not to the extent that suggests the Puebloans were suddenly refugees fleeing real or perceived outside danger. If they had been fighting with one another, then one assumes that only the losers would have sought refuge in exile. If anything, given the duration of their occupation of the region and the size of the late San Juan population, the Puebloans of the Great Sage Plain could be said to have lived fairly peaceful lives, at least in comparison to life as we know it today.

The "Great Drought" explanation for the movement of all Puebloans from the San Juan River basin continues to be the focus of archeological research. The dryland farms depended upon precipitation, not irrigation, for moisture. The tree-ring record indicates that a relatively severe drought began in 1276 and continued for two decades. The assumption is that drought reduced the productivity of the local soils to the point that the population was forced to move elsewhere to survive. The fact that the four latest tree-ring dates obtained from area structures, including Hovenweep Castle, are from 1277 to 1281, lends credence to the drought-caused emigration theory.

"They weren't traveling because there were droughts or there was pestilence. They were traveling because they were looking, searching, for the center place. Each one, until they found their

own center place, moved every four years . . . And they moved in any direction, any direction, with all kinds of languages."

--Edmund Ladd, Pueblo Indian scholar from Zuni Pueblo. The Anasazi: Why Did They Leave? Where Did They Go? 1991

However, a significant study conducted by archeologist Carla Van West raises questions about the drought theory in its most simplistic form. Her research focused on a large area of the Great Sage Plain including Cutthroat Castle just east of the Square Tower Community. Van West specifically examined the effect of drought upon the major soil types of McElmo Dome and compared that to varying population estimates for the area. She concluded that the drought alone would not have reduced soil productivity and crop yields to a level below that needed to adequately support even the largest estimated population.

Drought may have compounded social and environmental problems that the residents of the Great Sage Plain experienced, problems that are not as visible in the archeological record, but drought alone did not force the people to move. Some archeologists point to arroyo cutting and a resulting lowering of groundwater levels as an environmental constraint on continued farming in the region. But arroyos occur in the canyon bottoms, which comprise less than 10 percent of the productive farmlands in the Great Sage Plain.

The question is, were the San Juan Puebloans forced to move at all? They may have moved because they wanted to move.

Late in the thirteenth century the populations of the adjacent Rio Grande and Little Colorado River basins began expanding faster than could have been supported by birth rates alone. Dispersed communities there were aggregating into larger towns than ever seen on the Great Sage Plain. New ceremonies may have been introduced into an increasingly elaborate religion in many Puebloan communities south of the San Juan River basin. Could the excitement of the new towns have exerted a pull that the San Juan Puebloans could not resist?

"You know my clan, which is now the Third Mesa Clan—the Greasewood Clan—traveled these lands with the Bow Clan, the Reed Clan, and the Roadrunner Clan. Our clan, the Greasewood Clan, is today in Hopi alluded to primarily as "Utes." I mean, it's because we stayed for a long, long time around these areas [in the San Juan region] and subsequently had an influx of some of the Ute people from farther north. We consequently achieved a lot of social affiliation with those people. And when we arrived back at the mesas of Hopi, we carried some of the knowledge of the Ute people . . ."

--Leigh Jenkins, Cultural Preservation Officer, Hopi Nation, The Anasazi: Why Did They Leave? Where Did They Go? 1991

By the year 1300 or shortly thereafter there were no Puebloan communities left in the San Juan River basin, and the communities of the Rio Grande and Little Colorado River basins continued to grow.

Non-Puebloan communities continued to frequent the San Juan River basin. The Utes did not give up hunting, gathering, and the seasonal round and take up agriculture until little more than a century ago. Ute bands continued to travel across vast distances in the Rocky Mountain region including the San Juan River basin. They continue today to hunt and gather important plants from the area. Hovenweep may be the Ute word for "deserted valley." Sleeping Ute Mountain, visible from Square Tower, lies within the boundaries of the modern Ute Mountain Ute Indian Reservation.

A little more than a century after the San Juan Puebloans moved away, the mobile Navajos and Apaches entered the San Juan River basin from the north. They are still here today. Navajos learned farming from the Puebloans. Puebloan structures may have inspired the architectural style of their hogans. Southern and western approaches to Hovenweep National Monument pass near small Navajo farm hamlets. It is thought that the Navajos in the Hovenweep area crossed the San Juan River in 1864, successfully seeking refuge from the U.S. Army and Kit Carson's scorched-earth campaign. The population of the Navajo Nation today is nearly 250,000, comprising a majority of the population of the San Juan River basin. Thus, the Navajo Nation now exerts a strong influence on life throughout the Four Corners region.

Less than a half century after Columbus landed on the shores of this continent, the first Europeans—Spanish explorers—were making contact with the Puebloan communities of the Rio Grande and Little Colorado. In 1596, the first European settlement was established at what is now called San Juan Pueblo on the Rio Grande. In the four centuries that followed, the flags of Spain, Mexico, and the United States have flown over the ancient Puebloan homeland.

Many attempts were made to eradicate Puebloan religion and lifeways. None has succeeded, though Puebloan religion and politics today reflect the reality of existing in two worlds, one Puebloan and the other European. The Puebloan cultures and civilization have survived because they are so deeply rooted in the land that gave them birth.

The Towers of Hovenweep are witness to an important moment in the long history of an enduring people who love the beauty of wildness, love the beauty of human community, and see no distinction between the two.

> *"I suppose tribes and archeology can become really viable partners, and I hope that the efforts of archeology truly represent the interests of the cultures these lands represent . . . now the cultural resources are everybody's heritage . . . We should be proud that we hold some of the richest archeological information right here in the Southwest . . . We're all in this together. The heritage that archeology reveals is your heritage as well as mine."*

--Leigh Jenkins

In 1974 the anthropology department of San Jose State University, California conducted an archeological survey of the 656 acres inside the Cajon Mesa units of Hovenweep National Monument. In 1990 Alpine Archeological Consultants, Inc. conducted an archeological survey of a 4,000-acre area adjacent to, but not surrounding, the Square Tower, Holly, Hackberry, and Cutthroat units. While doing a survey, teams of archeologists record on maps all tangible surface sites within the area being inventoried and assign dates to the sites based on ceramics, stone tools, and architecture visible on the surface. The summaries of sites included here are taken from the 1974 and 1990 survey reports.

Adams, E.C., The Origin and Development of the Pueblo Katsina Cult. University of Arizona Press, Tucson.

Adams, K.R., 1992. The Environmental Archeology Program. In The Sand Canyon Archeological Project: Progress Report, William D. Lipe, editor, Occasional Paper Number 2. The Crow Canyon Archeological Center, Cortez, Colorado, p. 99–104.

Adler, M.A., 1990. Communities of Soil and Stone: An Archeological Investigation of Population Aggregation Among the Mesa Verde Region Anasazi, A.D. 900–1300. Unpublished Ph.D. dissertation. Department of Anthropology, University of Michigan, Ann Arbor.

Adler, M.A., and M.D. Varien, 1991. The Changing Face of Community in the Mesa Verde Region, A.D. 1000–1300. Paper presented at the Anasazi Symposium, Mesa Verde National Park, Colorado.

Baars, D.L., 1983. The Colorado Plateau: Geologic History. University of New Mexico Press, Albuquerque.

Cushing, F.H., 1974. Zuni Breadstuff. Museum of the American Indian. Heye Foundation, New York (Reprint).

Dozier, E.P., 1970. The Pueblo Indians of North America. Holt, Rinehart, and Winston, Inc., New York.

Fetterman, J., and L. Honeycutt, 1986. The Mockingbird Mesa Survey. Cultural Resource Series No. 22. Bureau of Land Management, Denver, Colorado.

Fewkes, J.W., 1925. The Hovenweep National Monument Annual Report. Smithsonian Institution, Washington, D.C., p. 465–480.

Greubel, R.A., 1991. Hovenweep Resource Protection Zone Class III Cultural Resource Inventory, Montezuma County, Colorado, and San Juan County, Utah. Prepared for and funded by the Bureau of Land Management, Colorado, Bureau of Land Management, Utah, National Park Service, Rocky Mountain Region. Alpine Archeological Consultants, Inc., Alan D. Reed, Principal Investigator, Montrose, Colorado.

Holmes, W.H., 1878. Report on the ancient ruins in southwestern Colorado examined during the summers 1875 and 1876. U. S. Geological and Geographical Survey of the Territories, 10th Annual Report. Washington, D.C., p. 383–408.

Hovezak, M.J., 1992. Construction Timber Economics at Sand Canyon Pueblo. Unpublished Master's Thesis. Northern Arizona University, Flagstaff.

Jackson, W.H., 1876. Ancient Ruins in Southwestern Colorado. U.S. Geological and Geographical Survey of the Territories, Annual Report 1874. Washington, D.C., p. 367–381.

Jenkins, L., 1991. On the Hopi View. In The Anasazi: Why Did They Leave? Where Did They Go? A Panel Discussion at the Anasazi Heritage Center, Dolores, Colorado. Southwest Natural and Cultural Heritage Association, Albuquerque, p. 31–33, 63.

Judge, W.J. (moderator), 1991. The Anasazi: Why Did They Leave? Where Did They Go? A Panel Discussion at the Anasazi Heritage Center, Dolores, Colorado. Southwest Natural and Cultural Heritage Association, Albuquerque.

Kenzle, S., 1992. Prehistoric Architecture: A Study of Enclosing Walls in the Northern Southwest. Master's Thesis in Progress. Department of Anthropology, University of Calgary, Alberta.

Ladd, E.J., 1991. On the Zuni View. In The Anasazi: Why Did They Leave? Where Did They Go A Panel Discussion at the Anasazi Heritage Center, Dolores, Colorado. Southwest Natural and Cultural Heritage Association, Albuquerque, p. 34–36.

Lipe, W.D., 1991. Chronology, Greater Four Corners Area. In The Anasazi: Why Did They Leave? Where Did They Go? A Panel Discussion at the Anasazi Heritage Center, Dolores, Colorado. Southwest Natural and Cultural Heritage Association, Albuquerque, p. 68–71.

_____1992 Comments on the Anasazi Origins Symposium Papers, fifty-seventh annual meeting of the Society for American Archeology, Pittsburgh.

Lipe, W. D., editor, 1992. The Sand Canyon Archeological Project: A Progress Report. Occasional Paper Number 2. The Crow Canyon Archeological Center, Cortez, Colorado.

Matson, R.G., 1991. The Origins of Southwestern Agriculture. The University of Arizona Press, Tucson.

Olsen, N.H., 1985. Hovenweep Rock Art: An Anasazi Visual Communication System. Occasional Paper 14. Institute of Archeology, University of California, Los Angeles.

Ortiz, A., 1969. The Tewa World. The University of Chicago Press, Chicago.

Parsons, E.C., editor, 1936, Hopi Journal of Alexander M. Stephen. Columbia University Contributions to Anthropology, nos. 23 and 24. Columbia University Press, New York.

Sando, J.S., 1976. The Pueblo Indians. The Indian Historian Press, San Francisco.

_____1982. Nee Hemish: A History of Jemez Pueblo. The University of New Mexico Press, Albuquerque.

_____1992. Pueblo Nations: Eight Centuries of Pueblo Indian History. Clear Light Publishers, Santa Fe.

Schroeder, A.H., 1967–68. An Archeological Survey Adjacent to Hovenweep National Monument. Southwestern Lore 33 (3 and 4). Colorado Archeological Society, Boulder.

Swentzell, R., 1992. Personal communication to Ian Thompson.

Tainter, J.A., and B.B. Tainter, 1991. The Towers of Hovenweep. Paper presented in the symposium "The Social Dynamics of Goods and Information: Archeological Perspectives," at the fifty-sixth annual meeting of the Society for American Archeology, New Orleans.

Thompson, I.M., 1986. Four Corners Country. Dick Arentz, Photographer. University of Arizona Press, Tucson.

Thompson, I.M., M.D. Varien, S. Kenzle, and R. Swentzell. Prehistoric Architecture with Unknown Function. In Anasazi Architecture and American Design, B.H. Morrow and V.B. Price, editors. University of New Mexico Press.

Van West, C.R., 1990. Modeling Prehistoric Climatic Variability and Agricultural Production in Southwestern Colorado: A G.I.S. Approach. Unpublished Ph.D. dissertation, Department of Anthropology. Washington State University, Pullman.

_____1992. The Heuristic Value of Estimates of Prehistoric Agriculture: A Case Study from Southwestern Colorado. Paper presented at the Third Southwest Symposium, Tucson.

Van West, C.R., and T.A. Kohler, 1992. A Time to Rend, A Time to Sew: New Perspectives on Northern Anasazi Sociopolitical Development in Later Prehistory. Paper presented at the conference on The Anthropology of Human Behaviour through Geographic Information, Santa Barbara, California.

Van West, C.R., and W.D. Lipe, 1992. Modeling Prehistoric Climate and Agriculture in Southwestern Colorado. In The Sand Canyon Archeological Project: A Progress Report, William D. Lipe, editor, Occasional Paper Number 2. The Crow Canyon Archeological Center, Cortez, Colorado, p. 105–119.

Varien, M.D., 1993. The Sand Canyon Project Site Testing Program, 1988–1991. Occasional Papers of The Crow Canyon Archeological Center, Cortez, Colorado.

Varien, M.D., W.D. Lipe, B.A. Bradley, M.A. Adler, and I.M. Thompson, 1990. Southwest Colorado and Southeast Utah Mesa Verde Region Settlement, A.D. 1100 to 1300. Paper presented at the Conference on Pueblo Cultures in Transition. The Crow Canyon Archeological Center, Cortez, Colorado.

Williamson, R.A , 1984. Living the Sky. The Cosmos of the American Indian. University of Oklahoma Press, Norman.

Wills, W.H., 1988. Early Prehistoric Agriculture. School of American Research Press, Santa Fe.

Winter, J.C., 1975. Hovenweep 1974 Archeological Report, no. 1. San Jose State University, California.

_____1976. Hovenweep 1975. Archeological Report, no. 2. San Jose State University, California.

_____1977. Hovenweep 1976. Archeological Report, no. 3. San Jose State University, California.

SUGGESTED READING

Ambler, J. Richard, 1977. The Anasazi: Prehistoric People of the Four Corners Region. Third edition. Museum of Northern Arizona, Flagstaff.

Brody, Jerry J., 1990. Anasazi. Rizzoli, New York.

Cordell, Linda S., 1984. Prehistory of the Southwest. Academic Press, Orlando.

Ferguson, William M., and Arthur H. Rohn, 1987. Anasazi Ruins of the Southwest in Color. University of New Mexico Press, Albuquerque.

Judge, W. James (moderator), 1991. The Anasazi: Why Did They Leave? Where Did They Go? Southwest Natural and Cultural Heritage Association, Albuquerque.

Lipe, William D. (general editor), 1992. The Sand Canyon Archeological Project: Progress Report. The Crow Canyon Archeological Center, Cortez, Colorado.

Lister, Robert H., and Florence C. Lister, 1983. Those Who Came Before. Southwest Parks and Monuments Association, Tucson.

Noble, David Grant, 1985. Understanding the Anasazi of Mesa Verde and Hovenweep. School of American Research, Santa Fe.

Ortiz, Alfonso, 1969. The Tewa World. The University of Chicago Press, Chicago.

Sando, Joe S., 1992. Pueblo Nations. Eight Centuries of Pueblo Indian History. Clear Light Publishers, Santa Fe.

_____1982. Nee Hemish: A History of Jemez Pueblo. The University of New Mexico Press, Albuquerque.

_____1976. The Pueblo Indians. The Indian Historian Press, San Francisco.

I am particularly indebted to Mark Varien, research archeologist at Crow Canyon Archeological Center and doctoral student at Arizona State University, who has spent countless hours with me at archeological sites across the Southwest explaining not only the sites but also the scientific theory and method employed in archeological research. Mark generously gave me access to his own ongoing research and writing and commented several times on this text. I am also indebted to Rina Swentzell, Pueblo Indian from Santa Clara and architectural historian, who has accompanied me to Hovenweep and other ancestral pueblos on the Great Sage Plain. Rina explained them to me from the perspective of Puebloan peoples. Hovenweep Superintendent Chas Cartwright took many hours from his busy schedule to visit sites with me and to comment on the text as it progressed. Chas contributed a great deal to this project, and his assistance was invaluable. At Mesa Verde National Park, Superintendent Bob Heyder, Jack Smith, Mona Hutchinson, Art Hutchinson, Don Fiero, Kathy Fiero, and Allan Loy all provided comments or other support. Victoria Atkins at the Anasazi Heritage Center/BLM helped locate much of the research literature used here. Bill Lipe of the Crow Canyon Archeological Center and Washington State University provided helpful suggestions and comments. Archeologist Carla Van West of Tucson provided her research materials and encouragement. Puebloan scholars Alfonso Ortiz, Edmund Ladd, Joe Sando, and Leigh Jenkins graciously allowed me to quote from their published works. My neighbors Jim and Betty Biggins provided a valuable lay perspective on the text. I am grateful to all the above individuals, and others too numerous to name, for their assistance. Any errors or misinterpretations contained herein are my own.

I.T.

1993

CANYONLANDS NATURAL HISTORY ASSOCIATION is a not-for-profit organization established to assist the scientific and educational efforts of the National Park Service (NPS), Bureau of Land Management (BLM), and the USDA Forest Service (USFS), agencies that together oversee more than 7.5 million acres of federal land in southeastern Utah.

Our goal is to enhance each visitor's appreciation of public lands by providing quality educational materials, both free and for sale, in our outlets in park visitor centers, other agency contact stations, and through our on-line catalog.

Our primary source of income is the sale of educational materials. All sales items must pass a rigorous review process managed by CNHA and our agency partners.

The funds we donate support agency programs in various ways, including seminars, outdoor educational programs, equipment and supplies for ranger/naturalists, exhibits, new facilities, and funding for research.

3015 South Hwy 191, Moab, Utah 84532
(435) 259 6003 voice
(435) 259 8263 fax; e-mail info@cnha.org;
website www.cnha.org

Established in 1967
Member of Association of Partners for Public Lands (APPL)

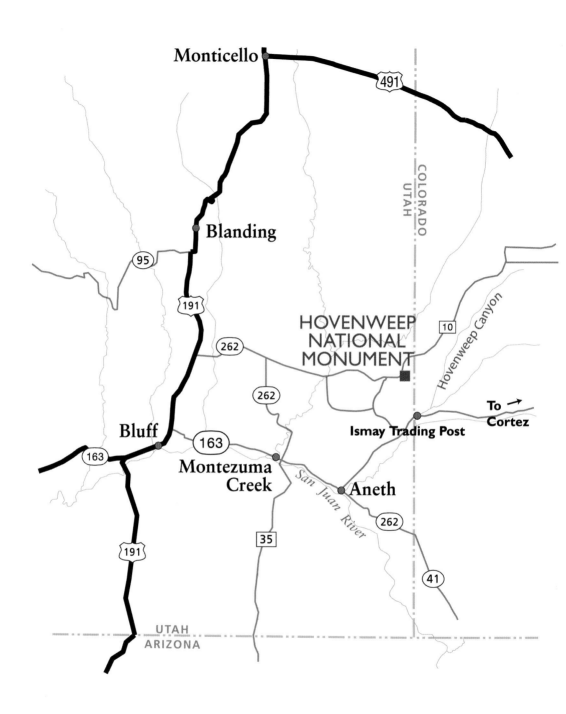